Sleep Kit
for Kids

Ahna de Vena

Gentle Crest Press
Sydney Australia

The Sleep Kit for Kids is designed to provide general information and guidance to help improve sleep. It is not a substitute for medical advice, or treatment. If your child has persistent sleep problems or other health issues, please seek support from appropriate healthcare services.

ISBN: 978-1-7635367-0-8

Copyright © 2024 by Ahna de Vena. All rights reserved.
www.ahnadevena.com

Sleep Kit for Kids

Book One
The Sleep & Dream Book　　　　　　　　　　8

Book Two
The Good Sleep Guide for Parents　　　　　35

Audio Download
Drifting into Dreamland Audio　　　　　　87

Progress Tracker
Checklist for Restful Nights　　　　　　　88

How to use this kit

Welcome! You're about to embark on a journey of positive change, bringing restful nights and brighter days for both you and your child. This kit will help support your child's natural ability to sleep well, while empowering you to create healthy sleep patterns and enhance well-being for everyone.

I'm Ahna de Vena, and I'll be guiding you step by step through this process—making it easier than you might expect.

Getting started

Start by reading the *Good Sleep Guide for Parents* (page 35). It's a quick read, and you can begin applying changes right away, then gradually build at a pace that suits everyone. The guide has three parts:

1. Support for you: Learn how to manage your stress and feel more at ease as you navigate these changes. This will also help you become a calming presence at bedtime.

2. Essential habits for good sleep: Discover simple, science-backed practices to reset your child's body clock and improve sleep.

3. Deepening your understanding: This section provides deeper insights and strategies to support your child's sleep and well-being.

Using the Sleep & Dream Book & Drifting into Dreamland Audio

Gently introduce *The Sleep & Dream Book* to your child (page 8). The book includes calming practices that help them relax and fall asleep. Read it at a pace that allows them to follow along and experience the soothing techniques. Encourage your child to discover their favourites.

If they're still awake, play the *Drifting into Dreamland* audio (page 87) as a soothing bedtime companion. I recommend using a dedicated screen-free MP3 player to avoid distractions from other devices.

Embracing the journey

Every step you take makes a difference, and though change may take time, the results will be deeply rewarding.

Use the *Checklist for Restful Nights* (page 88) to track your progress and celebrate every win—big or small.

You've already taken the most important first step towards transforming bedtime into a comforting and positive experience. Here's to peaceful nights, happier mornings, and a journey full of gentle growth!

the Sleep & Dream book

*for the tender child
inside us all*

I'd like to show you a special place	12
The softness game	14
Bubble breath	16
Your peaceful place	18
Your heart friend	20
Making friends with the dark	22
A kind voice in your head	24
Ride the waves	26
Watching your thought clouds	28
The thank you channel	30

I'd like to show you a special place

There is a whole world inside you.

A world that is yours, and only yours.

It's a special place, where you can rest, and dream, and create anything you want.

Wonderful things happen when you spend time inside yourself.

That's why I made this book for you.

When I was young, the outer world was sometimes scary and hard for me.

So, I made my inner world a comforting place. Then I felt more peaceful and could sleep easier at night.

As you read this book, you'll learn new ways to explore your inner world.

Always remember, this adventure can be just as you want it to be.

Shall we go together now, to your inner world?

The softness game

When you're in bed, softness is all around you, and you can feel snuggly, like a caterpillar in a cozy cocoon.

If you're a bit wiggly and awake—you can play the softness game.

Do you want to snuggle into softness?

Feel the softness of your pillow.
Let your head relax into the softness a little more.
Feel the softness of your bed.
Let your whole body relax into the softness a little more.
Feel the softness of your sheets.
And your pyjamas on your skin.
Feel everything that's soft, and stay with the softness.
Mmmmmmmm
As other thoughts come in, play the game again.
Feel the softness, of your pillow, your sheets, your pyjamas.
Feel the softness with your whole body,
and see if you can stay with the softness a little more.

Bubble breath

Have you noticed that your body breathes without you doing anything?

I like feeling the flow of breath that's always coming and going all by itself.

See if you can watch your body breathing right now, in and out, in and out, in a steady rhythm.

You can also do fun things with your breath.

My favourite is blowing slow bubbles. It makes my heart smile, and I'd love to do it with you!

*Close your eyes and breathe in gently through your nose.
Make a small circle with your lips, keeping them soft.
Breathe out slowly through your lips until all your breath is gone,
and imagine you're blowing bubbles into the air.
Breathe in gently through your nose,
then breathe out slowly through your lips, blowing bubbles.
Keep breathing gently in through your nose,
and out through your lips, slowly blowing bubbles,
and imagine them floating away.*

Your peaceful place

It's a good idea to make a peaceful place in your inner world.

A place that's yours, where you can go whenever you want.

It could be a place in nature like a beautiful beach with gentle waves, a sunny garden with soft grass, or a fluffy white cloud in a blue sky.

Or it might be a one-of-a-kind place that's only in your imagination.

You can make your peaceful place just as you want it to be.

It's okay if you don't see pictures in your mind. Just imagine the feeling of being in your peaceful place and your feelings will take you there.

Close your eyes and let your whole face be soft.
Imagine your peaceful place.
What is it like? What sounds do you hear?
What are you doing? How do you feel?
Take as much time as you need.
Stay in your peaceful place as long as you like.

It's your secret hideout.

A place you can go whenever you want.

All you have to do is close your eyes and imagine you're there, in your peaceful place.

Your heart friend

Imagine having someone who's always there when you need them. Someone very kind who comforts you.

You can have this heart friend in your inner world.

My heart friend is tall and gentle with big, soft wings that lovingly wrap around me at night as I go to sleep, and whenever I need to feel safe.

*Close your eyes and imagine a friend you would
love to have with you always.
Imagine they are with you now.
How do you feel?*

You can hold a pillow close and imagine it's your heart friend.

Or put a pillow against your back and imagine your heart friend is with you.

If you have any worries, you can whisper them to your heart friend.

Your heart friend is always here for you.

Making friends with the dark

I used to be afraid of the dark. I'd lie in bed and imagine things that made me scared, then I couldn't sleep.

I knew the dark was always going to be part of my life, because night-time comes at the end of every day.

So I decided to make friends with the dark.

And guess what I learned? The dark is really magical—because it can contain anything. It all depends on what I think about.

What do you like about night-time?

Do you like the stars shining above you and the moon glowing in the sky?

Do you like the sound of insects singing and the breeze in the trees?

Do you like lying down and feeling cozy before you sleep?

Maybe you like to imagine comforting things, like soft angel wings wrapping around you.

When it's dark, you can think about what you like about night-time, and fill the dark with things that help you feel peaceful.

Like twinkling stars, gentle moonlight, and soft angel wings.

Then the dark can be a friendly place.

A kind voice in your head

Have you noticed there's a voice in your head?

Does that voice say mean things sometimes?

When I was young, people said mean things to me, and then I heard mean voices in my head.

It was a big relief when I stopped listening to those mean voices.

I made kind voices in my inner world, which I could listen to instead. Then my inner world was a more comforting place.

You can do the same if you like.

When you hear a mean voice in your head, here's what you can try:

Say "I'm not listening to you."
Then think of something a kind friend would say.
Choose kind things you like to hear.
Keep repeating them until you feel calm.
If the mean voice returns you can say:
"I'm not listening to you."
Then repeat kind things a good friend would say.

You can make your inner world a place that has voices you like to hear.

Ride the waves

Feelings come and go, just like waves in the ocean.

You can feel happy one minute and sad the next. You can feel calm, then all of a sudden upset.

Feelings like happiness and love, are gentle waves.

Feelings like fear and anger, can be big rough waves.

When waves come (especially big ones), here's something you can do...

Put one hand on your belly and one hand on your heart.
Let out a big sigh ahhhhhh. Feel your hands on your body.
Notice how your body feels. Is it tight or soft? Warm or cool?
What else are you feeling right now?
Everything you're feeling is okay.
If you start thinking about something else,
just notice your hands on your body, and what you're feeling right now. Everything you're feeling is okay.

You are the ocean not the waves.

You can ride the waves.

Watching your thought clouds

When you're in bed, your thoughts can go all over the place.

You might think about what happened during the day, or what you'll do tomorrow, or many other things.

Then it can be hard to fall asleep.

Your thoughts are like clouds.

You can let them come and go just like clouds come and go in the sky.

Imagine a big blue sky full of clouds.
Some are light and fluffy. Some are heavy and grey.
You're just watching the clouds.
As they float across the sky, and fade away.
Keep watching the clouds as they come and go.

Whenever you notice your thoughts going all over the place, imagine a sky full of clouds, and see if you can let your thoughts be clouds.

Just watch them, coming and going, and fading away.

The thank you channel

I used to think about things that made me sad, angry or worried. Then I discovered I could think about things that made me smile instead.

It's like changing channels in my head, like changing channels on the TV, or opening a different app.

Do you ever feel upset about something, and then keep thinking about it over and over again? You'll feel better if you switch to the Thank You channel. Here's what you can do if you want to try:

Think of something you feel thankful for.
It can be anything, like the air you're breathing.
The sun or stars in the sky.
Your soft pillow, or a good friend.

Think about anything you feel thankful for.
Then whisper a quiet "thank you" in your inner world.
Notice how you feel when you quietly say "thank you."
You might feel like smiling.
And the smile might spread through your whole body.
And you might think of other things you feel thankful for.

Sometimes when you try to switch to the Thank You channel, you might not feel happy, and that's okay. Just feel what you're feeling and ride the waves as best you can.

The Thank You channel is always here, when you're ready to try again.

Give yourself a cuddle

I hope you've enjoyed exploring your inner world.

Now you know many ways you can comfort yourself. Whatever happens in the outer world, you always have your inner world to come home to.

Keep exploring your inner world as often as you can, and you'll make new discoveries.

Always remember there's only one YOU.

And you are precious.

Spending time in your inner world, is like giving yourself a cuddle.

I'm sending you a gentle cuddle now...

the Good Sleep Guide for Parents

Part 1. Your child's sleep begins with you

An invitation 41
Your mood matters 42
One-minute mood-shifters 44
Your ultimate calm reset 49
Using *The Sleep & Dream Book* and audio 52
Embracing positive change 55

Part 2. Essential habits for good sleep

Simple sleep science 58
Light wakes us up 60
Darkness – Nature's sleeping pill 63
The essential morning habit: Say hello to the day ... 65
The essential evening habit: Quiet time 67
Taming the great sleep destroyer 68
Making your home sleep-friendly 70

Part 3. Deepening your understanding

Sleep cycles are good news 76
Naps – How to use them wisely 79
How much sleep does your child need? 80
Planning is your friend 83
Nourishing tips for good sleep 84
The gift of healthy sleep 86
Drifting into Dreamland audio download 87
Checklist for restful nights 88

1

Your child's sleep begins with you

An invitation

You're about to discover how to transform sleep for everyone in your household.

Quality sleep brings far-reaching benefits—from boosting overall health to enhancing focus, emotional balance, and cognitive function. When your child sleeps well, it supports healthy brain development, strengthening their ability to learn and grow. Improving their sleep could be even more powerful than hiring a tutor!

By following the guidance in this book and avoiding shortcuts, you'll be amazed at the changes you can create. Within just a few weeks, you could be walking out of your child's room in as little as ten minutes, knowing they'll fall asleep independently.

Think of this as a sleep reset—an investment in a few weeks that will pay off for years to come in ways beyond what you can imagine.

Feeling sceptical? That's okay. Those feelings often stem from past experiences, and the past is as close as yesterday.

Right now, I invite you to focus on the book in your hands and open the door to new possibilities. With just a few adjustments to your mindset, daily habits, and nighttime rituals, you'll be encouraged by how quickly your child can naturally settle into deeper, more restful sleep.

Your mood matters

How you feel affects everyone in your family. That's why caring for yourself before tending to others' needs is so important.

Kids are like sponges—they pick up on everything you're feeling.

Your emotions are expressed through your facial expressions, tone of voice, posture, and movements. You are the most significant part of their environment, which is why your mood matters.

When you're feeling frazzled in the evening, shifting your state should be a priority. It doesn't have to take an hour or be a big deal. Sure, a bath or massage every night would be nice, but who has time for that?

So, I'm going to give you some one-minute mood-shifters. Once you practice these skills for a while, you'll feel confident in your ability to regulate your emotions and be a calming presence at bedtime.

These mood-shifters will become your go-to helpers, wherever you are—in the kitchen, on a bathroom break, or even while driving. For example, using them on your commute home can help lift your mood before you walk through the door.

Try just one, or string them together. If you've had a rough day, you might want to do all five!

In the beginning, take a little time to practice—just a few minutes here and there when you're not too tired or under pressure. Then you'll have these tools in your pocket, ready to use when needed.

One-minute mood-shifters

These simple, yet powerful practices can help shift your mood anytime you feel anxious or stressed, activating a relaxation response in your body and mind.

If bedtime is usually stressful, these techniques can help change that pattern. At first, you may only experience brief moments of calm, but with regular use, you'll start noticing longer-lasting periods of ease. Over time, your habitual reactions to bedtime will soften, making the process feel smoother and more manageable.

Remember, change is gradual. Even a 1% improvement is progress worth celebrating, as small shifts compound over time. With consistency, these practices will become second nature, as effortless as breathing or smiling.

While these techniques are great for resetting your mood in the moment, they aren't a substitute for addressing deeper, underlying issues. If bigger challenges are at play, seeking additional support might be necessary to work through them.

Long out-breath

An extended exhalation activates your vagus nerve, which switches on the relaxation response throughout your entire body. Your heart rate will calm, your breathing will become easier, adrenaline and other stress hormones will decrease and you'll think more clearly.

Bring your attention to your breathing.
Let your out-breath be a little longer than usual.
Let the in-breath come naturally.
Soften your face, shoulders, chest and belly.
Keep letting each out-breath be a little longer than usual,
in a gentle, non-forceful way.

Mona Lisa smile

When you smile, your brain recognizes the expression and then releases feel-good hormones like endorphins, serotonin, and dopamine. Even a tiny smile like the Mona Lisa's does the trick.

Bring a little smile to your lips.
Let the corners of your eyes lift a little too.
Breathe easily, and continue to smile like the Mona Lisa for at least a minute.
If your smile gets bigger—go with it and enjoy!

Inner kindness

We all have an inner critic—the voice that can be harsh or judgmental. This practice helps you develop a kind inner voice to replace those critical thoughts, softening your inner experience and fostering more self-compassion.

Say something kind and encouraging to yourself.
Something a good friend might say, like:
"It's okay. Everything you're feeling is okay. Just be here.
You'll get through this. This will pass."
Repeat kind and encouraging phrases until you feel more at ease.

Thought switch

Thoughts activate hormones that influence how you feel both mentally and physically. By switching your thoughts, you can shift your body chemistry and improve your mood.

Gently notice any thoughts.
Ask yourself, "Are these thoughts taking me in a direction that feels good?"
If the answer is no, blink your eyes a few times and change your body position.
Now, switch your thoughts to something calming and positive.
Like something you're thankful for.
Starting a new activity can help maintain the switch.

Calming body pause

When your attention feels scattered, use your body as an anchor to come home to yourself. By focusing on your body in any moment or situation, you simplify everything, reduce stress and gain a healthier perspective.

Bring your attention to your body.
Notice everything you're in physical contact with, and how the contact feels.
Feel the weight of your whole body.
Notice how gravity is gently pulling you toward the earth.
Be gentle and inclusive as you pay attention to what you're experiencing right now.
Notice your predominant physical sensation.
Gently focus on your body as best you can for at least a minute.

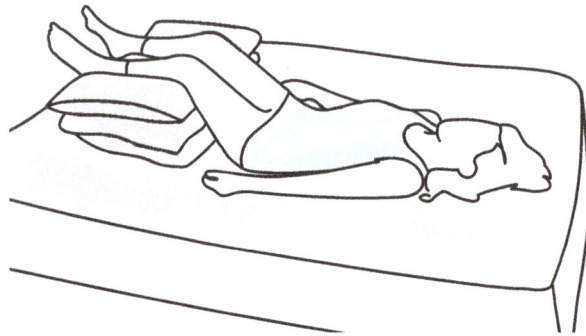

on the end of a couch

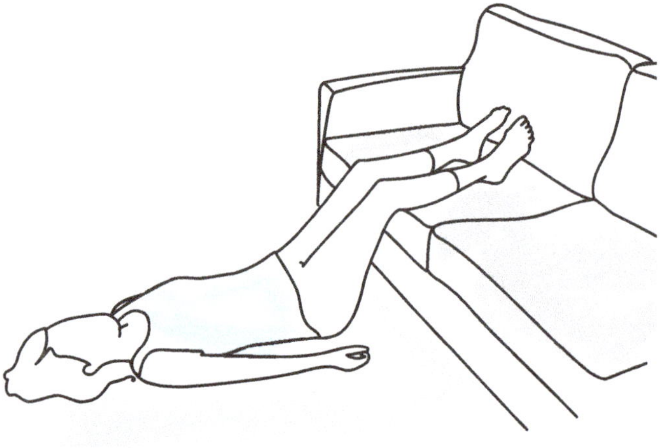

on a couch seat

on a bed with pillows under calves

Your ultimate calm reset

When you need more than a one-minute mood shifter, use the ancient practice of elevating your legs. This gentle inversion can swiftly transform exhaustion and overwhelm into a state of calm and refreshment in just ten minutes.

By boosting blood flow to your upper body, this practice calms your entire system, including your adrenals and heart rate. It also helps slow racing thoughts, eases back pain and regulates blood pressure.

One of the greatest benefits is how it resets your nervous system. Elevating your legs activates the body's natural 'rest and digest' mode, leaving you feeling steady, clear-headed, and ready to keep going with a calm energy if you need to.

It's as simple as getting into a comfortable position and letting gravity do the rest.

Evenings can be tough, but pushing through fatigue isn't the answer. Instead, take a ten-minute break, elevate your legs and feel revived. You'll gain the energy and patience to enjoy the rest of your evening.

Practicing this regularly can significantly reduce stress and help you feel more balanced and refreshed.

Whether you need a revitalising break or a way to unwind before bed, elevating your legs is the perfect solution—it might even become a family favourite everyone can benefit from.

You'll find comfortable options in the diagrams and detailed instructions on the following page.

How to Elevate Your Legs

To get the most out of this practice, choose a restful place with a comfortable surface to lie on and find a support for your calves. If needed, adjust the height of the support with cushions or folded towels.

Move your hips slightly away from the support until your body feels completely at ease. Use the diagram as a guide, and avoid having your thighs at a 90-degree angle to your back, as this can create tension.

If you feel tension in your neck, place a small folded towel under the top of your head to help lengthen and relax your neck. Comfort is key.

Set a timer for 10-25 minutes, so you can fully relax without checking the time. This will help you fully relax. To help you settle, consider listening to soothing instrumental music, which is less stimulating than music with lyrics.

Ensure your phone is on airplane mode so you can rest deeply without interruptions.

This simple practice provides both instant and long-term benefits. It's hard to believe something so easy can be so life-changing, but it really is.

Try it once, and you'll be hooked.

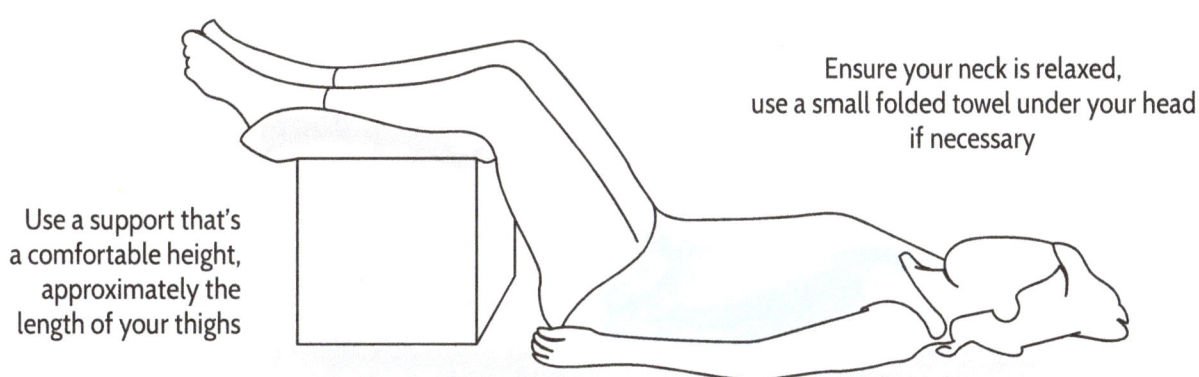

Using The Sleep & Dream Book and audio

Take some time to gently introduce *The Sleep & Dream Book* to your child. Read it at a pace that allows them to follow along and experience the calming practices. Check-in along the way, helping them find their favourites. Encourage your child to explore the practices in their own way, giving them space to experiment. Over time, they'll build the confidence to use these skills independently—empowering them to fall asleep on their own.

You could start with this bedtime ritual: Read one storybook followed by *The Sleep & Dream Book*. Read at a relaxed pace. If they're still awake at the end, play the *Drifting into Dreamland* audio. This can become their comforting bedtime companion, allowing them to fall asleep to the soothing voice—freeing you from having to stay in the room.

If your child is still awake after you've left the room, don't worry. It may take time for them to get used to the new resources. Be patient and encouraging to help them adjust.

Some children will love the audio immediately, while others may need more time and encouragement. For example, one child initially resisted, but after just one week of gentle encouragement, fell in love with it and began asking for it every night.

When your child isn't listening to the audio, encourage them to self-soothe and practice their new sleep skills. You might pop in and say, "Remember you can play the softness game" or whichever is their favourite.

As your child's inner world strengthens, you'll both experience more independence and freedom.

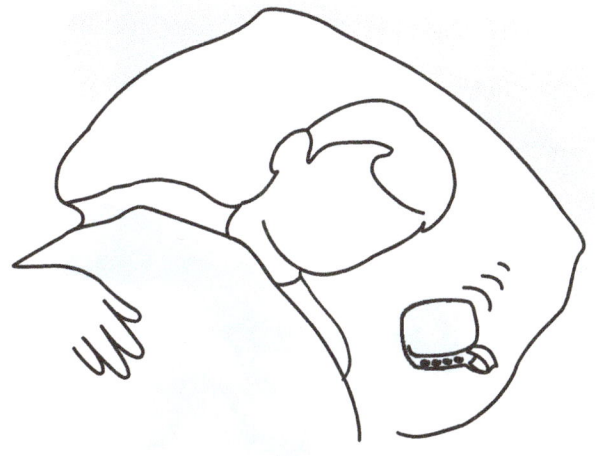

Embracing positive change

Change can be uncomfortable because we all have a creature of habit inside who likes things just as they are. When you try to make changes, that creature often resists with thoughts like, "I don't want to do this," "This is too hard," or "This won't work for me." But with consistent effort, new habits become easier, and eventually, even the creature of habit settles into new ways.

Implement changes gradually and gently. Take the pressure off.

For example, you can start with a single adjustment, and once that feels stable, add another. Progress may happen quickly or slowly, but little steps in the right direction will get you where you want to go.

Change isn't just about action—it's about mindset. We're constantly mentally rehearsing what's ahead by anticipating how things might unfold. Why not let mental rehearsal work for you by picturing restful nights and easier bedtimes?

As you envision these changes, also allow space for whatever comes up along the way. Frustration, doubt, and discomfort may arise—and that's okay. Hold yourself with tenderness as you navigate these moments, and stay present with the process, trusting that every small step matters. The more vividly you can imagine and feel the change, the more your mind, body and actions will align with it. Your imagination and expectations play a powerful role in shaping reality, so open up to the possibility of more restful sleep for both you and your child.

It's easy to forget where you began, so keep track of your progress by jotting down your bedtime experiences and reflecting weekly on how far you've come. Celebrate every win, no matter how small. If doubts arise, looking back will remind you of all you've already achieved

Change is a journey, not an instant fix, so appreciate each step you take.

2

Essential habits for good sleep

Simple sleep science

Our bodies follow a natural 24-hour sleep-wake cycle. This cycle is regulated by our internal body clock—a region in our brain known as the suprachiasmatic nucleus (SCN). The SCN controls the production of two key hormones: cortisol and melatonin.

Cortisol, produced by the adrenal cortex, is our "get-up-and-go" hormone. We need high levels early in the day to feel alert and motivated. Without enough cortisol early in the day we can feel sluggish and half-asleep.

An early morning peak in cortisol is essential not just for waking up but also for setting an internal timer that triggers melatonin production later in the evening.

Melatonin, produced by the pineal gland, is our "rest and restore" hormone. It initiates the sleep process and helps us fall asleep and stay asleep. To feel sleepy at bedtime, we need adequate melatonin levels.

Light and darkness are the environmental cues that trigger these hormones.

Light exposure in the morning boosts cortisol production, while darkness in the evening signals melatonin production.

To promote healthy sleep patterns for your child, managing exposure to both natural and artificial light is key.

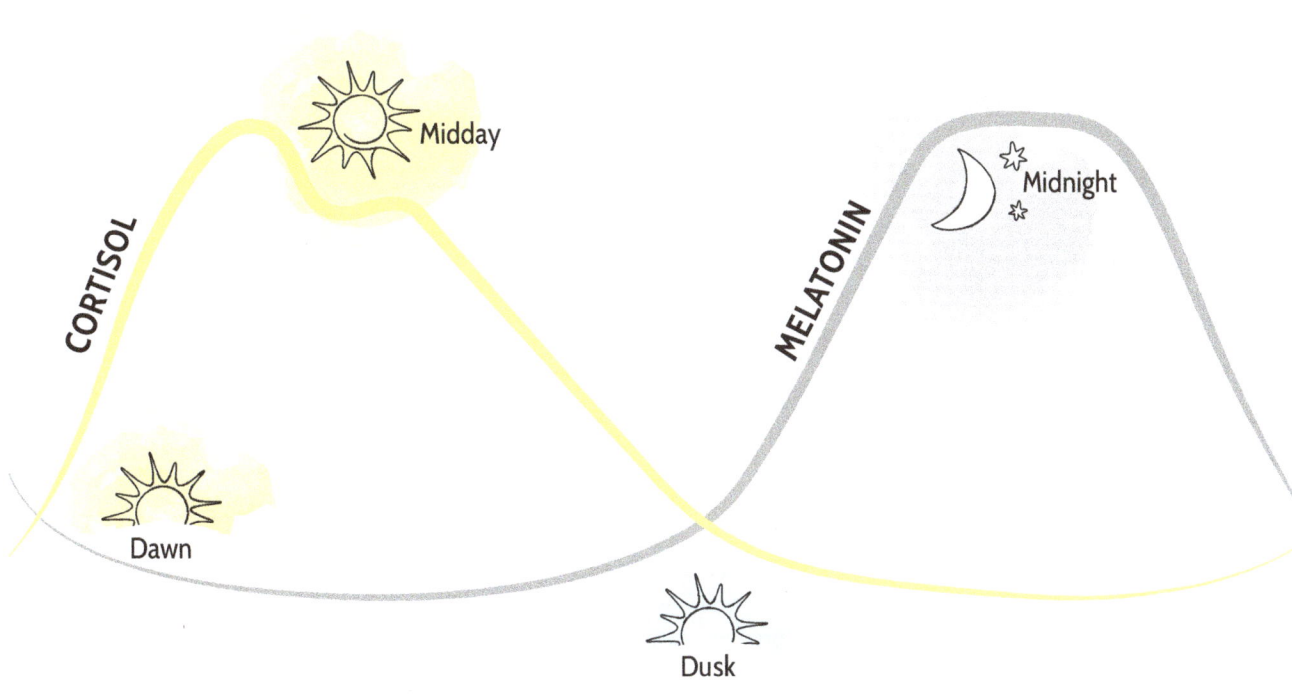

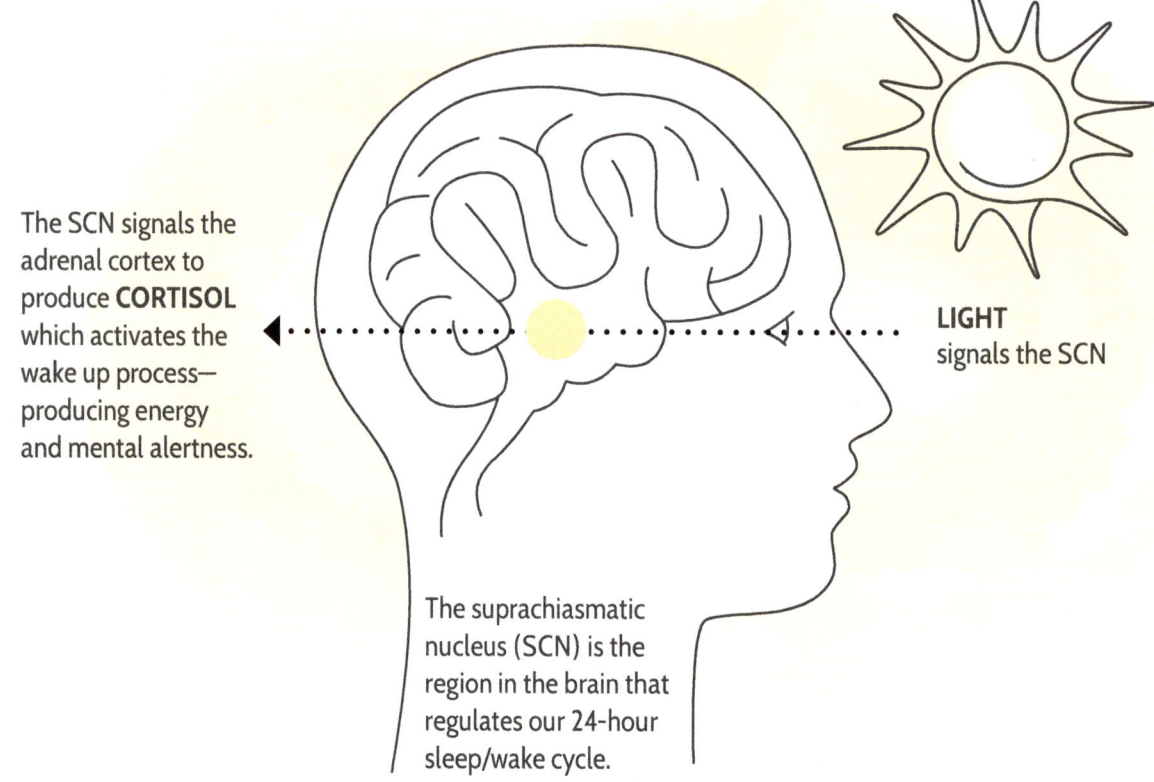

Light wakes us up

Light is a powerful stimulant that directly impacts our body chemistry and mood.

When light enters our eyes, it's detected by specialized brain cells called retinal ganglion cells. These cells send signals to the SCN, which then instructs the adrenal cortex to produce cortisol—our primary wakefulness hormone.

This is why light is an even better stimulant than caffeine!

To feel alert and motivated throughout the day, we need exposure to bright, full-spectrum light early in the morning.

Unfortunately, many of us spend too much time indoors and miss out on this vital sunlight. Lack of natural morning light slows down our metabolism, makes us feel tired, and reduces our motivation.

Lucky for us, it's easy to get into an energizing morning groove. Simply step outside with your child and say hello to the day.

Morning sunlight not only boosts wakefulness but also sets the stage for an easeful bedtime. An early cortisol peak influences the evening as well; about 12-16 hours after this morning spike, the body naturally starts producing melatonin, preparing for restful sleep.

Darkness – Nature's sleeping pill

Darkness is a natural sedative that calms our system and promotes sound sleep.

When our eyes detect low light or darkness, retinal ganglion cells signal the SCN (suprachiasmatic nucleus), which then instructs the pineal gland to produce melatonin—the hormone that makes us feel sleepy.

This is why creating a low-light environment in the evenings is so important. It allows the body to undergo the hormonal shift needed for quality sleep

The problem is, darkness has become increasingly elusive.

Before the invention of the lightbulb, people naturally fell asleep shortly after dusk, as they couldn't simply flick a switch to turn night into day. Now, artificial light sources flood our evenings, disrupting natural sleep patterns.

Exposure to artificial light at night interferes with both falling asleep and staying asleep.

To support smoother bedtimes, dim the lights in your home well before bedtime and use amber bulbs (which emit no blue light) whenever possible. This helps your child's body produce the melatonin they need to feel sleepy, fall asleep, and stay asleep—allowing you to rest better too.

By reducing light exposure and limiting screen use in the evening, you'll create an environment that promotes quality sleep and overall well-being for everyone.

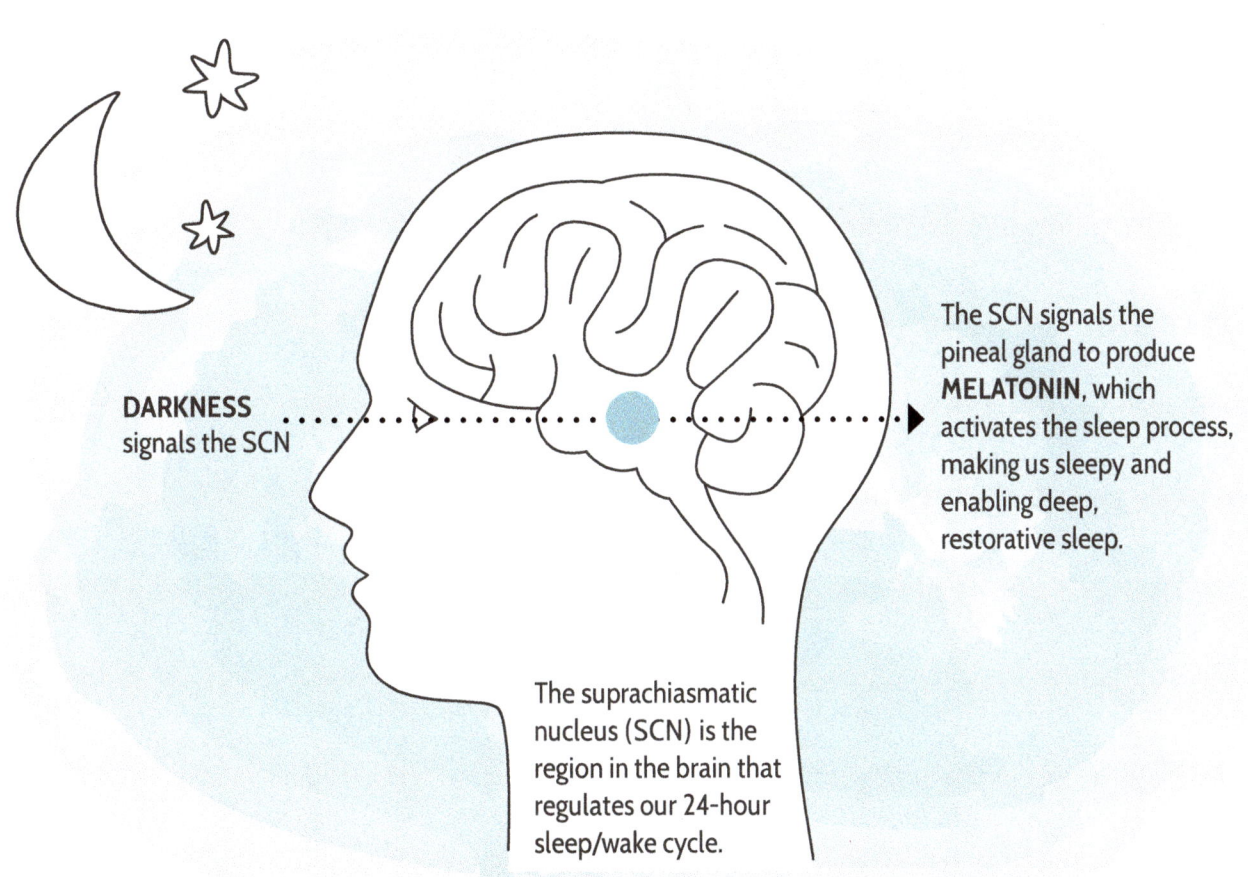

The essential morning habit: Say hello to the day

To ensure your kids have the energy and alertness they need throughout the day, take them outside for 5-10 minutes every morning and say hello to the day.

The simple habit of early morning exposure to full-spectrum light has been shown to regulate both cortisol and melatonin release, leading to more daytime alertness and healthier sleep patterns.

Simply go outside, find a sunny spot and turn your faces to the sun.

If it's sunny, ten minutes is enough, but if it's cloudy, stay outside for at least fifteen minutes. Going for a morning walk or getting new toys for the yard can help establish this habit.

It's important to note that sitting indoors near a window isn't enough.

The intensity of natural light measured in lux (a unit of light intensity), outside under the sky, is at least 50 times stronger than the light indoors. We need outdoor light to instigate a cortisol peak. If you can't access the outdoors, purchase a full spectrum lightbox.

Taking your kids outside early each morning and saying hello to the day will positively impact their physical and mental well-being as well as their sleep.

The essential evening habit: Quiet time

To create an environment that promotes calmness and sleep, it's essential to minimize light exposure and stimulation at least 30-60 minutes before bedtime. You can think of this as an "electronic sundown" when you switch gears and transition into quiet time. Here are some suggestions to help you do this:

- ⟩ If it's still light outside, pull curtains and blinds to darken your home.
- ⟩ Use lamps with amber globes instead of overhead lights.
- ⟩ Notice your internal pace and shift into a slower, quieter way of being.
- ⟩ Turn off all screens. The blue light they emit disrupts sleep by suppressing the production of melatonin.

By implementing these changes, you'll create a supportive bridge between wakefulness and sleep.

The subdued lighting and slower pace will signal your child's body to stop producing stimulating cortisol and start producing calming melatonin, promoting a peaceful night's rest.

Making these changes may be challenging at first. But it's worth the effort to create a peaceful transition to sleep. If you face resistance, hold the boundary firmly and kindly. Eventually, everyone will adjust to the new routine.

Once everyone gets accustomed to this quiet time, you'll all benefit from improved sleep and reduced stress. Your firm commitment to these changes will make them work for the entire family.

Taming the great sleep destroyer

Currently, 70% of children use electronic devices or watch television before bed, which can lead to delayed sleep onset, shorter sleep duration, and daytime drowsiness (Lund et al., 2021). Children are particularly sensitive to blue light from screens, which disrupts melatonin production, making it harder to fall asleep and affecting sleep quality.

Just 30 minutes of screen time in the evening can increase alertness, making it harder for kids to fall asleep and significantly affecting their sleep quality.

Additionally, excessive screen use can contribute to emotional challenges like anxiety and depression, which further disrupt sleep. To minimize these harmful effects, experts recommend:

- Stopping the use of electronic devices 30-60 minutes before bed.
- Keeping all screens out of the bedroom.

Establishing firm boundaries with device use, particularly in the evening, is key. This may require staying strong in the face of resistance. Remember, behaviour change can feel uncomfortable at first but gets easier with time.

By consistently maintaining these supportive habits, your family can enjoy a more relaxed bedtime routine and a smoother transition to sleep. While these changes may seem drastic, they are vital for improving bedtime and sleep quality for you and your loved ones.

THREE KEY SCREEN HABITS FOR RESTFUL SLEEP

1. Establish an electronic sundown before bedtime.

Commit to winding down with quiet activities in dim lighting at least 30 minutes before bed.

2. Enjoy screen-free wind-down rituals.

Engaging in calming, screen-free activities helps children prepare for restful sleep. Options include taking a bath in subdued light, gentle stretching, drawing, listening to calming audiobooks or music, and having peaceful conversations or shared storytelling.

3. Establish a clear rule: no devices in bedrooms at night.

Blue light from screens disrupts melatonin production, leading to poor-quality sleep. To prevent screen overuse and promote better sleep, keep all electronics, including televisions, out of the bedroom. A practical solution is to store devices in a safe or locked cabinet overnight.

Making your home sleep-friendly

Making a few simple adjustments to your home environment can significantly improve your family's sleep quality. You can take these steps at your own pace and enjoy discovering new ways of living that feel good for you and your family. Even implementing just one change can have a positive impact and provide support for your bodies to unwind and switch hormonal gears in the evening.

Create soft lighting options throughout your home

You'll be surprised at how much more relaxed everyone feels when you minimise the light in your home after sunset. This is one of the most beneficial things you can do to support your family's natural ability to sleep well.

- 〉 Use amber or low-wattage globes where possible.
- 〉 Use lamps instead of downlights. The light receptors in our eyes are designed to respond to light from above (the sun). We're less stimulated by lights situated low.
- 〉 Gradually turn lights off throughout the night until there's just one dim light in each room.
- 〉 Use the light above the stove or a lamp in the kitchen after dinner.
- 〉 Use small nightlights for the bathroom and hallways.
- 〉 Ensure all bedrooms have an amber lamp.

Amber globes are a supportive addition to your home as they create a restful ambience that mimics candlelight. They are free of blue light, which makes them helpful to have all around the house, and excellent in bedrooms as the last light before sleep. You can find "no blue light bulbs" by searching online. Amber globes are worth the investment as they promote quality sleep for your entire family.

Keep bedrooms cool and dark at night

For optimal sleep, the body needs to lower its temperature by one or two degrees, regardless of age. Here are some tips to create the right environment:

- Minimise the use of heaters in bedrooms to avoid overheating
- Choose bedding that keeps the body cool but not cold. Keep an extra blanket handy if needed, but avoid using too many layers, as overheating can disrupt sleep, especially for children.

Reduce light exposure in bedrooms:

- Avoid leaving any lights on in the bedroom while sleeping. If your child is afraid of the dark, consider using a red night light or an amber globe in the hallway to provide a gentle sleep-friendly glow.
- Use heavy curtains or blinds to block outside light. For best results, position them outside window frames to prevent light from leaking in.
- For some children, using a soft eye mask at bedtime can be helpful.

Limit harmful frequencies while you sleep

We are constantly surrounded by invisible frequencies that can negatively impact our health, but because we can't see them, we often overlook their effects. Children are especially vulnerable, as their skulls are thinner and their brains are still developing. While some exposure to these frequencies may be unavoidable during the day, we can take steps to reduce exposure and protect our health while sleeping.

Electromagnetic fields (EMFs) are emitted by power lines, household wiring, appliances, and microwaves. Additionally, cell phones, cell towers, and wireless internet connections emit radiofrequency (RF) radiation.

WiFi, in particular, generates a significant amount of electromagnetic radiation, as it is designed to transmit large volumes of data. Prolonged exposure to the frequencies emitted by phones, tablets, and computers can be especially harmful to children, whose bodies and brains are still developing.

A 1997 Australian Senate Discussion Paper highlighted the importance of reducing electro-pollution in our bedrooms. Researchers found that even low-level exposure to electromagnetic fields—at frequencies as low as 50-60 hertz—can significantly reduce melatonin production.

Melatonin is a vital sleep hormone that not only regulates sleep but also helps detoxify the brain and reduce inflammation, both of which are essential for maintaining optimal health. Supporting the body's natural melatonin production is crucial, especially for children. However, administering melatonin supplements to children is not recommended, as early studies suggest it may potentially affect the timing of puberty (Jenni OG et al. 2005, Urbanski HF et al. 2006).

KEY STEPS TO REDUCE HARMFUL FREQUENCIES

1. Set a timer on your WiFi modem to automatically turn off while sleeping.

2. Use a battery-operated alarm clock and keep phones out of bedrooms.

3. Charge all electronic devices outside bedrooms to reduce exposure to electromagnetic radiation.

3 Deepening your understanding

Sleep cycles are good news

A night of sleep isn't one continuous event; it unfolds in cycles that last about 90 minutes. This is good news! It means waking during the night doesn't ruin sleep—as long as it's handled in a way that allows for an easy return to slumber.

Each sleep cycle consists of five stages, each characterized by different brainwave activity and other biological changes. As shown in the diagram, a lot happens in our bodies during sleep, both neurologically and physically.

For babies and young children, sleep cycles are shorter than 90 minutes. By age three, they're typically around 60 minutes long, and by age five, they extend to the 90-minute cycle that remains consistent through adulthood.

Understanding that we all sleep in cycles can help you feel more at ease about waking in the night.

Each night, we typically go through five to nine sleep cycles. It's normal to wake briefly at the end of a cycle, often without even noticing. Sometimes we wake fully, and staying calm—knowing it's natural—makes it easier for both you and your child to fall back asleep.

The amount of deep sleep and REM sleep we get varies based on age, health, and lifestyle. Younger children require more deep sleep for healthy growth and development, making it crucial to establish good sleep habits that support this.

The diagram illustrates a typical 90-minute sleep cycle.

STAGE 1	STAGE 2	STAGE 3	STAGE 4	STAGE 5
Light Sleep A light sleep that's easy to awaken from.	**Transitional** A more stable sleep than light sleep. Body temperature drops. Brain chemicals block the senses, making it difficult to be woken.	**Deep Sleep** Breathing slows. Muscles relax. Growth hormone is released. Tissue growth and repair occur. Brain waves are extremely slow. This is the most restorative stage of sleep.	**Transitional** Transitional sleep is repeated.	**REM Sleep** Rapid Eye Movement (REM). The body becomes immobile. Eyes dart back and forth. The brain is active and dreams emerge. Mental rejuvenation occurs during REM.
Slowing brainwaves 7 cps (cycles per second)	**Fluctuating brainwaves** 3-14 cps	**Very slow brainwaves** 0.3 cps	**Fluctuating brainwaves** 3-14 cps	**Fast brainwaves like wakefullness** 5-40 cps
1-7 mins	15-20 mins	20-40 mins	5-20 mins	1-10 mins

ONE SLEEP CYCLE

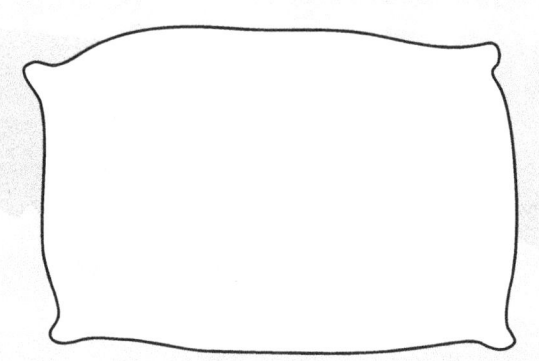

20 minutes ✓
60 minutes ✗
90 minutes ✓

Naps – How to use them wisely

Daytime naps can improve children's nighttime sleep, but it's important to align naps with their natural sleep cycles. To do this, wake your child from a nap before they enter deep sleep (around 20-25 minutes) or at the end of a full sleep cycle (about 90 minutes). Waking them after an hour can leave them feeling cranky or groggy, as their brain slows to deep, restorative sleep at this stage.

In a nutshell: 20 minutes great. 90 minutes great. 60 minutes no good!

Naps act as powerful resets, preventing overtiredness and enhancing nighttime sleep quality. When children become overtired, their bodies release stress hormones, making it harder for them to fall asleep later.

A well-timed nap can reduce overstimulation, helping them unwind and relax more easily in the evening. Think about how hard it is for an overtired child to settle down. Napping before they reach that point can make all the difference for the rest of the day—and night.

Even a short 20-minute nap, taken anytime before 3pm can transform their mood and sleep quality.

As children grow, continuing to provide quiet recovery time during the day remains essential. Many cultures embrace the universal need for rest with a daily siesta. By allowing time for recovery, children's bodies and minds can function at their best.

So, make time for naps. Just 20 minutes can make a world of difference to your child's day and night— for the better.

Note: Suggested nap times are relevant for children aged five and above.

How much sleep does your child need?

Adequate sleep is vital for your child's well-being. Before adjusting their sleep duration, it's best to establish the essential morning and evening habits.

Once a regular sleep and wake routine is in place, you can gradually adjust their sleep duration to better meet their needs. When your child's body is in sync with natural light patterns and their cortisol and melatonin levels are balanced, they'll naturally sleep for the right amount of time.

To determine how much sleep your child requires, consider their age and overall health—younger children need more sleep. Use the recommended sleep times chart as a guide.

Be mindful of your child's bedtime. Even small changes can significantly impact their health, development, and learning.

Calculate how much sleep they currently get, and divide it by 90-minute increments (the length of a sleep cycle for children aged five and older).

Gradually adjust their sleep duration to match the recommended amount for their age, rounding up to the nearest 90-minute increment. For example, if your child sleeps for eight hours, try extending their sleep to nine hours (six cycles), and assess how they respond. If more sleep is needed, extend it to 10.5 hours (seven cycles). Make sure you're calculating sleep from the moment they actually fall asleep, not just when they go to bed.

Understanding your child's sleep needs will help them get the rest they need to thrive.

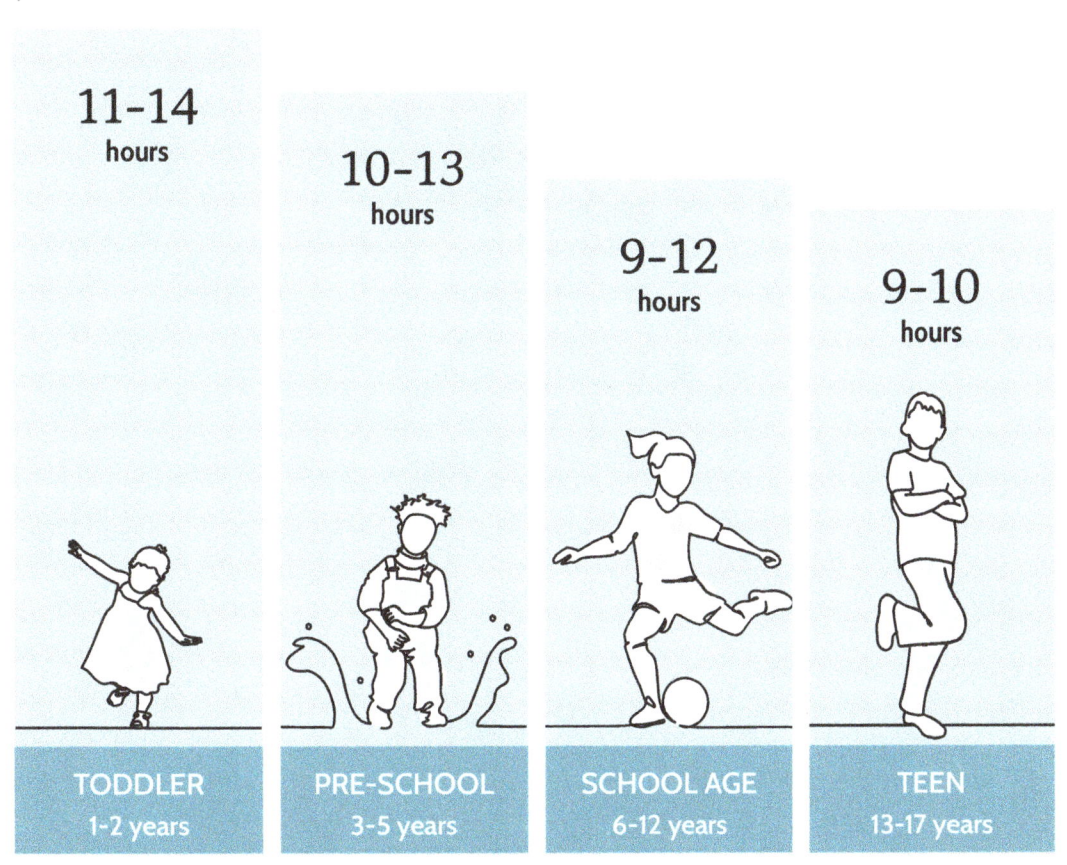

Planning is your friend

What's the secret to a smooth evening? Planning ahead.

The most helpful things to plan are dinner, your child's bedtime, and your own bedtime. These are the cornerstones of your evening routine. While other tasks may come up, these three are the foundation.

When planning your evenings, work backward from when you and your child need to be asleep. Then, decide when to start quiet wind-down time and dinner. By planning, strategising, and allowing for a little flexibility, you can make the transition to sleep easier for everyone in your home.

Remember, planning doesn't take away spontaneity—it provides a framework to work within.

For example, one busy parent of three shared how she and her kids create a weekly meal plan on Sunday mornings. They choose meals the kids can help prepare, which has been a game-changer for her. She shops once a week using a waste-free list, removing the stress of daily dinner decisions and last-minute trips to the store.

The alternative to planning is "winging it," which often results in chaos and stress. The hours between sunset and bedtime are precious. How will you use them? Planning helps you feel calmer and more in control, giving you the freedom to bond with your family, unwind, or engage in nourishing activities. A simple plan ensures you make the most of this valuable part of the day.

Nourishing tips for good sleep

What kids eat and drink throughout the day—not just in the evening—can greatly impact their ability to fall asleep and stay asleep. While there's no one-size-fits-all diet for perfect sleep, a balanced diet full of nutrient-dense foods and limited processed foods is essential. Here are some helpful tips:

Water is life

Dehydration can cause various issues in the body and brain, including sleep disturbances. Children should drink about 30ml of water per 1kg of body weight each day, and even more if they are sweating or losing fluids. Incorporate good quality water (filtered or spring) into their morning routine, and make sure they stay hydrated throughout the day. However, avoid giving them water close to bedtime to reduce the chances of waking up during the night.

Sugar and high carbs are sleep hazards!

High sugar and carbohydrate intake are linked to more frequent night awakenings and less deep sleep. These foods cause a spike in blood sugar, followed by a crash, creating an up-and-down effect that impacts mood, energy, and sleep quality. Be cautious with high-carb meals, energy drinks, sugary beverages, and fruit juice, as they can disrupt sleep.

Protein and healthy fats are key

Protein and healthy fats are crucial for promoting good sleep. Protein plays a vital role in various bodily functions and cellular processes. Without adequate complete protein intake, children may experience physiological stress, making it harder to sleep well.

Good sources of complete protein include fresh fish, free-range eggs, high-quality meat, chicken, and full-fat dairy (for those who tolerate lactose). For vegetarians, combine foods like rice and legumes, to get complete proteins.

Healthy fats are a great energy source, support brain development and help stabilize blood sugar, making them an ideal snack for kids. Swap out high-carb and sugary snacks for options like coconut, full-fat yogurt, feta cheese, butter, ghee, olive oil, edamame, eggs, oily fish (like tuna), ripe avocado, sunflower or pumpkin seeds. Ensure seeds are fresh and stored in the fridge to prevent mould.

Great snack options for kids include sugar-free, full-fat yoghurt or coconut yogurt with a bit of fruit, cookies made with real butter and unrefined sweeteners, and mashed avocado with tuna and mayonnaise on a cracker. These options provide protein and healthy fats to support sustained energy during the day and promote better sleep at night.

The gift of healthy sleep

Congratulations on making it to the end! You've taken meaningful steps that will enhance both your child's well-being and your own. In a world that often overlooks the value of deep, nourishing sleep for our health and happiness, you've chosen to prioritise one of life's greatest gifts.

I hope this book has sparked a deeper appreciation for the power of sleep and equipped you with the knowledge to nurture it in your home.

Remember, we all have a natural ability to sleep well.

By fostering this gift, we unlock the full potential of our bodies and minds, gaining more energy, focus, emotional balance, and joy.

As you turn this final page, know that prioritising sleep is one of the most loving and impactful choices you can make for yourself and your family. By nurturing and protecting the gift of deep, restorative sleep, you'll transform not just your nights, but every moment of your lives.

Drifting into Dreamland

AUDIO DOWNLOAD

Imagine your child gently drifting off to sleep, feeling calm and comforted. Inspired by the principles of the Sleep & Dream Book, this soothing audio creates a peaceful bedtime experience with a calming voice guiding your child into dreamland.

Download here: **sleepkitzzz.com/ka**

To get the most out of this audio, I recommend using a dedicated, screen-free MP3 player and keeping all other devices out of the bedroom.

Checklist for restful nights

- **Emotional regulation**
  Learn practical skills to manage your emotions and be a calming presence in the evening. This will also help you navigate the process of change with more ease.

- **Morning sunlight**
  Take your child outside each morning to greet the day and absorb natural sunlight.

- **Supportive hydration and nutrition**
  Keep your child hydrated and ensure they get enough protein and healthy fats throughout the day. Avoid refined sugar, especially in the evening.

- **Soft lighting**
  Close blinds and use amber or small night lights to mimic natural, calming firelight.

- **No screens in the bedroom**
  Remove all screens (such as TVs, tablets, and phones) from your child's bedroom. This helps you monitor screen use and supports a healthy screen sundown.

- **Screen sundown**

  Turn off all screens at least an hour before bedtime to enable the hormonal shift to melatonin, which prepares the body for quality sleep.

- **Quiet time**

  Establish quiet time in low light 30-60 minutes before bed to help your child unwind.

- **Calming bedtime reading**

  Read *The Sleep & Dream Book* slowly, allowing your child to follow along. Over time, you can guide them spontaneously once you both know the skills.

- **Drifting into Dreamland audio**

  Play the audio on a screen-free speaker to help your child fall asleep independently.

- **Keep going!**

  Celebrate every small improvement as you and your child adjust to these new habits on the path to consistent, restful nights.

About Ahna de Vena

My passion for improving sleep began with my own childhood struggles with insomnia and anxiety. Enduring sleepless nights into adulthood led to significant health challenges and fueled my determination to find a solution.

Immersing myself in the study of natural medicine, I eventually reclaimed my ability to sleep well, transforming my life in the process. This journey inspired me to develop a holistic approach to sleep therapy, working privately with individuals and families, and presenting my corporate program globally.

For over 22 years, I've dedicated my career to helping people of all ages achieve better sleep and cultivate inner calm through natural methods.

Motivated by a desire to support children affected by trauma, I created sleep kits and began donating them through my charity, The Sleep & Dream Foundation. The positive results and enthusiastic feedback inspired me to make these kits available to everyone.

In a world that prioritises outer achievements, it can be challenging to slow down, quiet a busy mind, and get the rest we need to live fulfilling lives. My wish is for you and your child to find restful sleep, so you can enjoy peaceful nights and vibrant days.

A percentage of the profits from this book go toward supplying sleep kits to children and families in need.

www.ingramcontent.com/pod-product-compliance
Lightning Source LLC
Chambersburg PA
CBHW061120170426

43209CB00013B/1614